# Is ELIJAH MUHAMMAD THE OFFSPRING OF MARCUS GARVEY & NOBLE DREW ALI?

By
**Nasir Makr Hakim**
(Minister of Elijah Muhammad)

Published by
**Secretarius MEMPS Ministries**
111 E Dunlap Ave, Ste 1-217
Phoenix, Arizona 85020-7802
Phone & Fax 602 466-7347
Email: secmemps@gmail.com
Web: www.memps.com

ISBN 10  1-884855-45-8
ISBN 13  978-1-884855-45-0

Printed in the United States of America

# DEDICATION


To all the Believers and Followers
of
Elijah Muhammad,
Messenger of Allah,
without whom, we as fractions
would have no expectation
of ever
becoming whole.


~ ~ ~ ~ ~


The
Messenger
is a Sword
In A Man's Hand

*~ Sayings of Elijah Muhammad, Vol. 3*

# TABLE OF CONTENT

# PREFACE

This book was produced from a previously introduced work titled, <u>The True History of Master Fard Muhammad, Allah (God) In Person</u>. It was an introduction to that book to lay the base for such a profound work at it was. To date, that book about the Saviour, Master Fard Muhammad, is considered the best written on the subject.

This book is the actual introduction of that book and is being re-released as a stand alone, because of the importance of countering the idea or notion that Elijah Muhammad or his teacher, Almighty God in person, Master Fard Muhammad, somehow borrowed their knowledge or were perhaps intellectual or spiritual offspring of previous contemporaries.

As the author of this book, I have fallen out of disfavor with many we all thought were Muslims, followers of Elijah Muhammad. In the early days of depending on various individuals for support in one form or another, their pragmatic modes of dealing with me, when it came to Elijah Muhammad's books and work, sometimes forced them to conflict between the principles taught by Elijah Muhammad and those instituted in nationalist, afrocentric, and pan-africanist camps.

Consequently, my so-called hard line positions was too much for their "foot in everybody's camp" pragmatism.  Once the issue of Elijah Muhammad's roots was seriously addressed without political correctness or favoritism, all of those who got hit barked.  My intent is not to attack the character or work of Noble Drew Ali or Marcus Garvey or their followers, but to lift the name of Elijah Muhammad, Messenger of Allah, with truth and the caliber of credit it commands.  He paid the price to stand alone without sharing what he has earned with no one.

To make it perfectly clear, I am making sure it is re-introduced with a simplified title that directly puts the question and the answer in perfect view.

**Minister Nasir Makr Hakim,**
*Founder, Messenger Elijah Muhammad Propagation Society*

# WE MUST KNOW WHAT WE TEACH OR BE FOUND LIARS

How can one teach the people to know that which they do not know themselves?  Is it not true that to teach the people one way or the other, without knowledge, about anything, one can be charged with lying to the people?  One cannot teach that which one does not know!

It is the burden of the scientist to factually discover, describe, explain and predict according to real propositions or laws.  As well, the extent to which a scientist comprehends the laws or principles governing the facts he or she has under study, is the gauge of his or her ability to determine the exact nature and function of what's being studied.  Surely, the capacity to understand may be greater than the demonstrated ability to explain, but the mastery to explain anything cannot go beyond one's insight into the laws and principles governing the thing.

The explanation of any reality depends on, and can be no better than, our understanding of that reality. Fundamental to understanding is knowledge. Flaws in knowledge must result in flaws in understanding. Such flaws will always be mirrored in our explanations of reality. This defective frame of mind filters what we see, how we see things and why we see things, which rules our actions.

It is well known that the world in which we live does not base its findings exclusively on reality or natural laws. One great indictment of "this world" is manifested through how it goes about proving conclusions. The scientists are constantly testing their hands at determining patterns, predicting those patterns, and modifying them for the eventual purpose of controlling them. If they "knew" or had concrete knowledge, studying them wouldn't be necessary.

They don't know, which is why "theories" are such a fundamental part of Western World thought. A theory is systematically organized knowledge applicable in a relatively wide variety of circumstances, especially a system of assumptions, "accepted" principles, and rules of procedure devised to analyze, predict, or otherwise "explain" the nature or behavior of a specified set of phenomena. Also, theory is an assumption or guess based on limited knowledge or information.

Living under the rule of other than our own kind and self for the past 6000 years has brought much misunderstanding, much not knowing and many theories that have been used in many places and the people have taken theories that have been used in many places. A theory is not true until it has been proven to be true.

It is no coincidence that earning the highest educational degree in the Western World, in most cases, requires writing a dissertation, which is a proposition maintained by argument, or a hypothetical proposition, especially one put forth for the sake of argument or one to be accepted without proof. When there is no proof, then sometimes, more often than not, the force of repetition stands with said writers as the equivalent of proof. To repeat certain statements while ignoring rebutting facts, is a sure method of carrying convictions to the minds of thousands. They play upon the mob psychology and produce the desired effect.

When it comes to the true history of Master Fard Muhammad, Messenger Elijah Muhammad and the Nation of Islam, in general, the above method has and is being used one hundred percent. The media engages in spreading lies and fabrications through the forms of newspapers, magazines, books, news casting by radio and television. This is not just being done by whites; however, blacks have and are doing their fair share.

The popular course of writing against the Nation of Islam, more particularly, Master Fard Muhammad is this: 1) initial writers publish works which include statements of suggestion or insinuation; 2) This possibility is then transformed into a theory with follow-up works and additional media sources; 3) further follow-ups try to make a fact out of the theory. 4) Based on 1, 2, 3, above, what started as an ill-intended desire, eventually is converted, in 4 or 5 transfigurations, to a so-called "well established fact."

Take for example, the various points of view passed down through history, which attempt to "explain" the origin of Master Fard Muhammad and the Nation of Islam. The obvious variations and often contradictions manifest a gross indictment of ignorance. Most of the writing springs from the 1930's and lays a foundation for the various perpetuated theories still alive in these modern times.

During the Great Depression, the urban ghettos of the northern United States were fertile ground for the development of new religious movements. Between 1900 and 1930 approximately 2,250,000 Blacks left the rural south; most emigrated to large northern cities. This growth represented an increase of over 400 percent in the Black population of the north; in Detroit, the increase exceeded 611 percent.

The industrialized north had been viewed by many as a land of abundance, holding the promise of a better standard of living, employment, and equality. Most Blacks however, suffered severe economic hardship during this period. Their sense of deprivation was intensified by the difficulty of adjusting to a new environment and inequalities they endured in the social realm. Economic pressure often moves individuals to focus on their religious faith with greater urgency, and in the ghettos this tendency not surprisingly took on political overtones. Blacks were beginning to emerge from the shadows of slavery, and their religion had, of necessity, always served a variety of functions. Indeed, Fauset hypothesized that Black Americans' traditionally high religious participation was in part the result of the lack of other channels open to them.

C. E. Lincoln's research suggests that religious movements provided Black Americans the opportunity to participate in an atmosphere free from embarrassment or apology, these were places where they may experiment in activities such as business, politics, social reform, and social expression.

As well, he maintained that participation was often motivated by a racial or nationalistic urge.

The absolute and relative deprivation suffered by Blacks during the Depression would have exaggerated these tendencies on a large scale. The first groups to crystallize out of this initial ferment were the Moorish Science Temple, led by Noble Drew Ali, and the Universal Negro Improvement Association (U.N.I.A.) of Marcus Garvey.

The Moorish Science Temple originated in 1913.  Its leader, Noble Drew Ali, preached a doctrine that included a strict moral code and linked religion to nationality:

Christianity 's for the European (paleface) Moslemism is for the Asiatic (Olive-skinned). When each group has its own peculiar religion, there will be peace on earth.

Salvation depended upon accepting a new nationality; followers became Moors. Although its central tenets were undeniably political, the group did not take political action. They stressed obedience and loyalty to the American flag, believed divine intervention would bring about the end of white rule, and therefore cultivated a political, peaceful adherence to the status quo. The primarily religious Moorish Science Temple did, however, initiate overt political statements on the part of Black religion, and as many writers, Black as well as White, are continually keeping alive, "laid the foundation" for the movements that followed it. Noble Drew Ali's death saw the Temple virtually disappear; in its place, a more political group emerged. Bear in mind that for an organization to have existed with various aspects identical does not mean that either was purposely design to serve as a spring board for similar organizations that followed.

The Universal Negro Improvement Association originated in 1916 and was perhaps the most popular "back to Africa" movement in American history. The Garveyites, as they were known, invested their money and energy into amassing a large commercial empire, the goal of which was to see Africa become the homeland of all Blacks. Like the Nation of Islam, the U.N.I.A. stressed Black independence through self-sufficiency. Indeed, Marcus Garvey himself originated the phrase "Up you mighty race, you can accomplish what you will," a rallying cry frequently used by the Muslims' Messenger Elijah Muhammad. The movement progressed to the point of electing a Liberian government-in-exile, even having its own representative to the League of Nations, but began to lose momentum when the President of Liberia understandably refused the U.N.I.A. entry to his country.   Marcus Garvey was exiled in 1927 and his movement then faded from prominence.

No doubt, that a shallow exercise in study will reveal that when you study any discipline from a comparative stand point, varying elements of the disciplines will have similar traits; however, to suggest that one is parented by the other or that one is the legacy of another, is to miss any possible margin of differentiation.  What would set them apart is the basis or objective for which each were created or established.  Out of a vacuum, anything can develop; yet, one thing is certain:  When an entity is spurned, intelligence dictates that to really ascertain the true essence of it, one must focus on at least three things:  The objectives of the entity, the time line associated with it, and its achieved accomplishments toward its objectives.  One could argue if whether or not Nobel Drew Ali and the Moorish Science Movement accomplished their objectives within the three years prior to the Garvey movement?  One could equally argue the same when it comes to Marcus Garvey and the U.N.I.A.

There appears to be a great inclination for new writers, journalists and researchers to draw from the work of previous writers, especially when it comes to the early days of the Nation of Islam, because cameras, reporters and media interviews were elements which were not as welcomed then as they are today; consequently, most of the lies, fabrications, theories and the like, had been manufactured in part by "Negro journalists" working for white media. In those days, to be the "only colored" journalist automatically meant that you had to be the one who went and got the story about "colored" people and it had to sell or that journalist wouldn't eat; consequently, when it came to the Nation, a group that wasn't always in the media's camera (especially Elijah Muhammad), access to the Nation was difficult; so, if you could get access to "them" or get an interview, you were almost guaranteed a grub steak. What suffered were the facts and since lies, fabrications and the like sold, that's what white media bought.  They didn't want the truth, because they were trying to discredit Elijah Muhammad and the Nation of Islam for all intents and purposes anyway.  The same bad information is still perpetuated to this very day.

Wallace D. Fard, later interpreted by members of his movement as Allah. Or the Great Mahdi incarnate, first appeared in Detroit in July of 1930. Little is known of his early life and his founding of the Nation of Islam; the information that does exist is vague and often contradictory. Complementary myths concerning Fard's ethnic origins are diverse.

Despite the writers' conclusion that information regarding the origin of the Nation of Islam's "founder," and/or his early life is often vague and contradictory, it doesn't stop them from raising their "don't know" (ignorance) to that of a "know."  A case in point: In what many perpetuators of what's passed off as a classic work on the Nation of Islam,

C.E. Lincoln notes...

"...that among them is "a legend" that describes Fard as a black Jamaican whose father was a Syrian Moslem, and one that reports he was a Palestinian with a long history of participating in racial agitation."

In terms of the role Fard was eventually to play in the Nation's theology, according to Hatim A. Sahib,

"...two "myths" stand out. To Elijah Muhammad (later the leader of the Movement), he declared himself a member of the royal dynasty of the Hashimide Sheriffs of Mecca, while to Elijah's wife, Clara, he apparently stated he was a member of the tribe of Koreish (the prophet Mohammed's tribe)."

The variations and contradictions are just as interesting if not saddening when reading "new" writings about a subject which has been raked over the coals so long, even a fool can tell that the majority of the writers just don't know and are "too educated" to admit it.

Morroe Berger writes,

"One of Drew's followers, according to 'some historians' of the movement, was a man known by the name of W.D. Fard or by several variants of it. Although Mr. Elijah Muhammad has told me that Fard never was associated with Drew, Fard did create his own sect, the Nation of Islam, or the Temple of Islam, from which the present "Black Muslims" directly spring....It was claimed that Fard was born into the Koreish, the tribe of Muhammad himself."

**Interview at the home of Elijah Muhammad, 1965 reveals:**

**Interviewer:** "I have read, Mr. Fard Himself, was He a member of Nobel Drew Ali's movement?

**Messenger:** No. He was no member.

**(I)** Or was He a follower or something?

**(M)** He's independent; He's not a follower of any of them, He's not.

**(I)** Was He associated in any way with Nobel Drew Ali?

**(M)** No.

**(I)** These reports then, so far as you are concerned, are incorrect?

**(M)** That right, He was no follower of Nobel Drew Ali; He's no follower of anyone. He's self independent. He's self independent. There's nobody for Him to follow.

**(I)** There's a book call, They Seek A City, written by Arna Bontemps and Jack Conroy, which stated it could be the case, and I just wanted to know from you what your thought of it?

**(M)** The writer didn't have an understanding, as with so many still writing; they don't have a good knowledge of what they write on the subject, but they want to hurry out with something.

**(I)** Have you read Mr. Essien Udom's book?

**(M)** I've read enough of that.

**(I)** What was your impression?

**(M)** We have some good in there, but I could easily classify him with the hasty writers. He's too hasty in what he wants to write, and probably would write correctly, but he wants to hurry and get [his work] on the market. [Also] Eric Lincoln, they both have very good things in their work, but show undeveloped knowledge of just what's what...

**End Interview**

Elijah Muhammad, Messenger of Allah, had permitted countless interviews, such as the previous one, to many journalists, and the majority of them, especially first time interviewers, almost always would ask about Master Fard Muhammad and His whereabouts; yet, it seems that there is a great appetite to settle with outside conjecture rather than what Elijah Muhammad tells them. The motivations vary depending on the person and the journalist's employer. What's so strange is that many of those who have been granted rare interviews are in fact the very ones perpetuating varying and opposite views of what they have received directly from Elijah Muhammad himself.

When you get at the root of all the opposition and make it bear witness to the truth of the Messenger, you have forced all the branches to do the same. For example, every Black opposer of Elijah Muhammad gets his or her idea of opposition from the whiteman of America. Now the white man has already borne witness to the truth, even though this is against his nature. Where does this leave his Black followers? Their ignorance makes them unqualified; yet, many of the opponents understand Elijah Muhammad's teachings, but for varying reasons, seek to mislead others. There are many Black writers who will admit the profundity of Elijah Muhammad's writings, which in actuality are directly from Master Fard Muhammad; still, they speak and write as though there is no greater knowledge beyond what they have gained, or are studying, that either comes from whites or distant sages from outside the country. They will even go so far as to seek out esoteric, mystical and theosophical systems, along with the respective sages of these bodies of knowledge, in a futile attempt of refuting Elijah Muhammad, which is the same as refuting Master Fard Muhammad.

Many attempt to pass their ignorance off as higher knowledge. Hakim Shabazz refers to Master Fard Muhammad as an Enigma, which means that which is puzzling, inexplicable or incapable of being explained or interpreted; so, despite the blatant acknowledgment of uncertainty, like many other writers, he ventures out to "explain" - in his own words - the unexplainable. To assist him in the impossible, he seeks the aid of another Black writer, Charles E. Marsh, who is author of From Black Muslims To Muslims: The Transition from Separatism To Islam. Just the title of his book, alone, strongly suggests that at one time the Nation of Islam wasn't Islamic, but separatist.  This helps clue us in on his intent to rationalize his idea by raking and scraping any tid bit of theory, inferences, or conjecture to prop up his conclusion, instead of permitting the evidence to dictate a conclusion.

Most of the Arab world, as well as whites in America, have used the false argument that the Nation of Islam are not "real Muslims." That they are not worshipping the "true Allah,"  that they have a manufactured version;  therefore,  when  characterizing them, the buzz-word "Black" is put before the word Muslim to signal this perpetuation; thus, the title "From Black Muslim to Muslim."  This as well is consistent with the overall 1975 transition from the way Elijah Muhammad taught and administrated the Nation of Islam, and the way his son, Wallace Muhammad, eventually steered the Nation.

Wallace Muhammad didn't believe that Master Fard Muhammad was Allah (God), which  was  contrary  to  Who  Elijah

Muhammad had said, believed and taught that He was. Thus, after 1975, and the coup (overthrow) of the Nation of Islam, the political "evolutionaries" went to work siccing attack dogs and the like to explain the "new" Nation of Islam. From this same vein came books which beard the same hypocrisy fathered by Wallace. This frame of mind is evident in the title: From Black Muslim to Muslim.

As previously mentioned, a very sly and deceptive alternative to directly refuting who Master Fard Muhammad was, was to subordinate and downplay the profundity of what He taught by putting Him either in the same category with contemporaries or developing theories to establish the notion that the Nation of Islam had antecedents: An occurrence or event proceeding another or the conditional member of a hypothetical proposition.

When looking for antecedents, no attempt seems to be as difficult to prove, yet advanced so much as that of trying to show that the Nation of Islam was a direct result of Noble Drew Ali and Marcus Garvey's movements. There is some evidence that all three had similarities when it came to the people for whom the movements served; however, are these similarities significant enough to serve as grounds for saying they are forerunners of each other? Emphatically NO!

Of course, this subject could be developed point by point to substantiate the overall point; however, it is very possible and judicious to adequately examine the foundation or contents of "the wash" which would relieve us of wasting so much time waiting until it comes out in the rinse.

Noble Drew Ali, founder of the Moorish American Science Temple (1913) acknowledges Garvey's influence on his movement. His book, The Holy Koran-Seven, is replete with the teachings of Garvey.

In these modern days there came a forerunner, who was divinely prepared by the great God-Allah and his name is Marcus Garvey...

The author came to this conclusion with a mere, single direct quote, in his 42 page book; yet, to tie the Nation of Islam and Elijah Muhammad into this proposition he writes,

"It has been suggested that Elijah Muhammad was an active member on the U.N.I.A. (as well as the Ahmadiyya Movement. We should also note that Elijah emphasized the writings of Maulana Muhammad Ali, the eminent Ahmadiyya scholar)."

Not only does Shabazz give no references regarding a so-called membership, other than a "suggestion," but he doesn't even tell you where the suggestion came from. One would get more than that from the grape-vine! He further seeks to rescue this conjecture by heaping on more conjecture by trying to associate Elijah Muhammad with the translator of the Holy Qur'an.

When referring to the Holy Qur'an translation by Yusuf Ali as well as Maulana Muhammad Ali, Elijah Muhammad would compare various translations of various verses and the respective translator's commentaries. What's odd is that Shabazz didn't include Yusuf Ali, for Elijah Muhammad emphasized his writings too, since Shabazz deems comparing the footnotes in the two translations of the Holy Qur'ans as "emphasizing." This is but another frail attempt at associating Elijah Muhammad with another group or person merely because their writings were comparatively analyzed. Interestingly enough, though, Elijah Muhammad, in referring to Maulana Muhammad Ali, he would do so for clarifying the fact that Muhammad Ali, founder of the Ahmadiyya Movement, wasn't who he claimed to be, such as the Mahdi. Still in the defense of Master Fard Muhammad and His proper identity, Elijah Muhammad used these people to clarify the truth and not to use them as spring boards for his teachings.

# Is Elijah Muhammad the Offspring of Garvey & Drew Ali?

Within the same paragraph of the above short and weak "premise" of his assertion, Shabazz summarizes,

"Both Noble Drew Ali and Elijah Muhammad were influenced by Marcus Moziah Garvey's nationalism and theology, they merely translated it into Islamic terms....

How could Shabazz summarize when he never presented any facts or support for the summary?  He did not point out one instance to support his assertion that Elijah Muhammad was "influenced by Garvey's nationalism and theology" to, "merely" as he so nonchalantly states, translate into Islamic terms.

One writer builds his conjecture and theory atop the conjecture and theories of former writers for the purpose of "explaining" better than the previous writer, but one thing is overwhelmingly consistent, none of them have furnished any evidence to show that they factually know the origin of Master Fard Muhammad, nor have they produced any evidence to support their claim that either Master Fard Muhammad or Elijah Muhammad, His Messenger, were associated in any way to the Moorish Science Movement or the Universal Negro Improvement Association. The fact that they can't explain, reasonably interpret and, mind you, are still puzzled as to Master Fard Muhammad's origin, is grounds to invalidate any of their conclusions; for in the field of logic, if one's premises are incorrect and/or faulty, then any conclusion arrived at is invalid or moot, to say the least.

You should expect to see many other books surfacing with the same intent of trying to subordinate Master Fard Muhammad to a "common man." This was one of the tactics used by the disbelieving, hypocritical son of Elijah Muhammad, Wallace Muhammad. History has borne witness that he did convince a great many followers of Elijah Muhammad, which could account for the Great Hypocrisy manifesting since 1975. Even before this phenomena, there was a great attempt at trying to discredit Master Fard Muhammad and Elijah Muhammad by

Malcolm X; however, he didn't get "his" thing off the ground, and as history has it, he didn't have a physical man-child to carry his seed into the future, which means his future has been terminated!  Even if he had 1000 daughters, they will never produce a seed. He does have one spiritual seed, you can recognize him by his work.

There are still other books, pamphlets and newspapers perpetuating the same incorrectness, and being passed off as the legacy of Elijah Muhammad and the Nation of Islam.

It is the epitome of ignorance to deny the truth of a matter and at the same time admit that you don't have the facts.  It is the height of folly when attempting to build an unsupported argument the size of a planet, then make an attempt at fitting it through a pin hole of speculation, theory, and conjecture.  There should be a law against elevating such ignorance to the level of scholarship.

One of the greatest published attempts at discrediting the Nation of Islam was initiated by Simeon Booker and Ed Montgomery.  Mr. Booker had written a book published in 1964, titled "Black Man's America;" wherein he stated that the Nation of Islam was founded by a "flimflam artist who served a 3-year sentence in San Quentin prison for a narcotics law violation."  This aspect is mentioned because the same lies, but more extensive, were published in the San Francisco Examiner in 1963.  In response to this poisonous venom which this snake, and those who helped him, spewed up about Master Fard Muhammad (Who in fact is Allah in Person and Who is the One and Only teacher of Elijah Muhammad), the Messenger publicly announced in response the following article and challenge:

# Is Elijah Muhammad the Offspring of Garvey & Drew Ali?

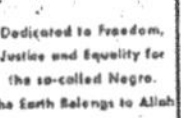

## Muhammad Speaks

Vol. 2—No. 24     AUGUST 16, 1963     111     15c—OUTSIDE ILLINOIS 20c

# Nation Of Islam Offers Hearst
# $100,000 To Prove Charge

## Beware of Phony Claims

### By Elijah Muhammad

I, Elijah Muhammad, Messenger of Allah, told the Los Angeles "Herald-Examiner" Office on Monday, July 29, 1963, that my followers and I will pay the Los Angeles "Herald - Examiner" Newspaper $100,000.00 (one hundred, thousand dollars) to prove the headline charge ("BLACK MUSLIM FOUNDER EXPOSED AS A WHITE") made against us; that we are following one Wallace Dodd w i t h many aliases including the name, Fard; that he is the man that I am representing to my people as being Master Fard Muhammad (Allah in Person) who appeared among us in Detroit, Michigan, in 1931 and is the same person (Wallace Dodd).

The Los Angeles "Herald-Examiner" also printed his prison history in San Quentin Federal Penitentiary on a charge of peddling dope, and that he admitted he was teaching us.

If he (Dodd) was teaching for money in those panic days in Detroit, he did not get it from us. Mr. Dodd, undoubtedly, must have b e e n teaching the white people if he received any money at all, because we did not have any.

WE DID NOT pay Mr. Fard any money to teach us and there are many who will verify this statement who are yet alive. We c o u l d hardly pay the rent of a hall in those days.

Sometimes they (the Be-

(Continued on page 3)

The Phony

The Savior

At left is the dug-up convict, Wallace Dodd, alleged by the sensation-seeking and anti-Negro white Hearst newspaper to be founder of the Nation of Islam in North America. At right, however, is the real and rightful Master Farad, of Mecca, who gave all to black people in America before returning to Mecca. The Honorable Elijah Muhammad has not only offered to confront the phony imposter invented by the Hearst press, but has exposed the deceit and has offered to pay $100,000 if they can prove their fraudulent claims. (See Mr. Muhammad's Column)

I, Elijah Muhammad, Messenger of Allah, told the Los Angeles "Herald-Examiner" Office on Monday, July 29, 1963, that my followers and I will pay the Los Angeles "Herald - Examiner" Newspaper $100,000.00 (one hundred, thousand dollars) to prove the headline charge ("BLACK MUSLIM FOUNDER EXPOSED AS A WHITE") made against us; that we are following one Wallace Dodd with many aliases including the name, Fard; that he Is the man that I am representing to my people as being Master Fard Muhammad (Allah In Person) who appeared among us in Detroit, Michigan, in 1931 and is the same person (Wallace Dodd).

The Los Angeles "Herald Examiner" also printed his prison history in San Quentin Federal Penitentiary on a charge of peddling dope and that he admitted he was teaching us.

If he (Dodd) was teaching for money in those panic days in Detroit, he did not get it from us. Mr. Dodd, undoubtedly, must have been teaching the white people if he received any money at all, because we did not have any.

WE DID NOT pay Mr. Fard any money to teach us and there are many who will verify this statement who are yet alive. We could hardly pay the rent of a hall in those days.

Sometimes they (the Believers) would give Him (Master Fard Muhammad) gifts such as topcoats, overcoats, ties, shirts, or a few packages of handkerchiefs—but money was so scarce in those days that we just did not have any.  Just about everyone who believes was on the "Relief" In Detroit Including myself.

I would like the Los Angeles "Herald - Examiner" to prove that this man (Dodd) was my teacher by bringing him to this country at our expense.

Mr. Wallace Fard Muhammad, Whom Praises are due forever, the Finder and Life Giver to we, the Lost Found Members of that great Asiatic Black Nation from the

Tribe of Shabazz, speaks 16 different languages. Can Mr. Wallace Dodd speak 16 different languages?

Mr. Wallace Fard Muhammad also writes 10 of the languages He speaks fluently. His native language Is Arabic (does Mr. Dodd speak Arabic?) of which we have in His handwriting and it is the best writing or penmanship In the Arab world.

Let Mr. Dodd prove that he was among us; prove that he gave us our names. Let Mr. Dodd prove who was his secretary and where were the Identification cards printed, of which we have with us today and did he write the Arabic on them himself?

If Mr. Dodd was The Mr. Wallace Fard Muhammad, why did not the F.B.I. arrest him for this teaching of truth? Let this paper prove these things before it headlines us as liars and worshippers of white devils.

I would like to ask the Herald Examiner to give us a minute close-up or this fake (Mr. Dodd) who they would like to make the public believe is our Saviour. Even the description of this man's height and weight does not correspond to Master Fard Muhammad's, (to Whom Praises are due forever) measurements. I know His height, His weight, the size of clothes and shoes.

WHEN MASTER Fard Muhammad left us, it was in 1934. Again, let Mr. Dodd prove that he and I were together and that the Lessons that I am teaching to my followers are from him, and where were they given to me and did he ever examine me on what he gave me, and where?

There are many questions that I could ask this Mr. Dodd about, that would prove to the world that this man is a fake that the Los Angeles "Herald-Examiner" has published. We believe this by the reasoning of such unfounded truth.

Let the Herald-Examiner Newspaper put us in contact with this Mr. Wallace Dodd.

We will show the world that the entire statement is false; that this Mr. Wallace

Dodd is not Master Fard Muhammad, To Whom Praises are due forever.

I HAVE warned you against allowing the devils to trick you into believing their false propaganda which they are spreading all over the world and especially among the so-called Negroes who have been the perfect model-slaves for 400 years and yet do not have freedom, justice, and equality from the slave-masters.

And now these smart, scientific tricksters are trying to prevent them from enjoying a permanent salvation that Allah (God), under the name of Master Fard Muhammad to Whom all Praises are due, has offered us.

We who believe in Him are a living proof of this offer that we are now being blessed with, even though we are afflicted with persecution and death.

You have those whom the Prophets prophesied of in Washington and in Rome (The Catholics) to deceive the whole world and especially the so-called Negroes.  Look

## Is Elijah Muhammad the Offspring of Garvey & Drew Ali?

In your poison book, the Bible, Revelation 12:9- 13:4, 8, 14- 14:11- 20:10 and 21:8.

# THE AUTHORITY TO BE AN AUTHORITY

For a good tree bringeth not forth corrupt fruit; neither doth a corrupt tree bring forth good fruit.  For every tree is known by his own fruit. For of thorns men do not gather figs, nor of a bramble bush gather they grapes. {Luke 6:43-44}

If I do not the works of my Father, believe me not.  But if I do, though ye believe not me, believe the works: that ye may know, and believe, that the Father [is] in me, and I in him. (John 10:37-38)

The above verses are excellent choices when laying a base and setting the tone for what I am attempting to illustrate here.  So many have and are presently trying their hands at defining, characterizing, labeling and explaining the origin of Master Fard Muhammad as well as who He is.

I, as well as the readers, must bear witness to the fact that if all of the afore-mentioned writers are using terms to describe their own assessment of the origins of Master Fard Muhammad with adjectives like enigmatic, obscure, baffling, puzzling, and mysterious, then the question must rise as to who actually KNOWS!  In mathematics we are taught that to understand the unknown, we must calculate on that which is known.

The above verses from the chapter of Luke recounts the words of Jesus wherein he says that "For a good tree bringeth not forth corrupt fruit; neither doth a corrupt tree bring forth good fruit."  The tree here represents something that is well rooted which serves as a producer or originator and that which something else comes from; the fruit represents the product.  The product of the tree has no choice as to what it is; for it is only a reflection or product of the tree.

Jesus illustrates with the above simile a relationship which is universal, meaning that in nature, new life is only a reproduction of the life before it.  All to say that a good tree can only bring forth good fruit and a corrupt tree will always bring forth corrupt fruit.

This principle is so consistent that Jesus goes on to say in the second verse, "For every tree is known by his own fruit. For of thorns men do not gather figs, nor of a bramble bush gather they grapes."  As this is so in nature and on the mundane or ordinary, earthly level, so it is on the spiritual level.

As the term "tree" is used to illustrate the origin of a fruit, the term "Father" is used the same; however, within the fruit lies a seed which can reproduce the tree, but not the fruit, because fruit comes from trees. We can't get fruit directly from seeds in most cases, there must be another stage such as a tree or vine.

In this case Jesus is referring to my "Father" in the same breath, in which he referred previously to the "tree."  Like the tree, the "Father," is the origin of offspring sometimes called fruit.  Only in this case, it is works which distinguishes from what "Father" or "tree" a product or offspring is from.  Therefore, when Jesus said, "If I do not the works of my Father, believe me not." Why?  It is because works, in this case, was the yard stick by which Jesus used to measure himself, with respect to the works the "Father" did.  His intent was to show that he either represented the Father or/and what the Father did is what he wanted to be measured by.

 Consequently, it was through this means of measurement which Jesus instructs that,"...if I do, though ye believe not me, believe the works: that ye may know, and believe, that the Father [is] in me, and I in him."  Thus, one would have to know something about the tree or the Father in order to adequately measure Jesus or the fruit.  This is where a reasonable degree of knowledge about nature and the scripture is absolutely critical and mandatory; whereas, to not possess this knowledge is to stand completely unqualified to speak one way or the other.

It was said that knowledge differs according to the capacity for it, according to the latent powers in a man.  Hence there is a variety of stages amongst Prophets and others.  Further progress is possible even beyond these stages, for divine knowledge knows no bounds. The highest stage is reached by one to whom all truths and realities are revealed untaught (not taught through scientist of this world's universities). This helps to explain why many of the writers who have attempted to explain Master Fard Muhammad have failed. As the Jesus said, "Ye are from beneath; I am from above: ye are of this world; I am not of this world." (John 8:23)

Is this not what Elijah Muhammad has been saying since he had come to public view and analysis? The real disposition, integrity and validity of this position is known only to him who enjoys it. We verify it by what some call faith, and by what is sometimes defined as reliance based on verifiable history.

I don't want the reader to misinterpret faith in this scenario with "belief." For it is so easy to associate terms with our relative or current usage, but I want to relieve the reader of too much personalization with these terms; therefore, permit me to define what I means as I go.

## Is Elijah Muhammad the Offspring of Garvey & Drew Ali?

Belief means to assent, to agree or to concur. Sometimes we will go along with a point, grant a point or give in to it or acquiesce. Why is it necessary to deal with this definition?  I am trying to illustrate a point here and that is for one to "just go along," then that's all it is or to "just to submit" doesn't mean you are convicted; one may just go along for an immediate benefit or favor.  We're still talking about "mere belief."  If I told you there is a 747 jumbo jet in your closet, you could exercise your choice to "believe" me, regardless of the motivation, you can just believe if you wanted to - right!  But what is it that makes us not want to believe that; what is it that inclines us to reject that?

Is it not so that our normal thought patterns produce certain probabilities which makes us prone to reject the fact that there is a jumbo jet in our closet?  Whereas, in our minds, we speedily weigh, analyze and deduct any probability, and even if we don't absolutely reject it, our general response will be rejection.  In our minds we have calculated the approximate size of a jumbo jet and the size of our closet and determine that such wouldn't fit, then we submit our finding as a rejection.  So, the question once again is what is the name of the process which we have just exercised?

There is a certain type of calculating which we as humans have come to rely upon, and it is that reliance which makes us different from the animals of the field.  We operate off projections of consistencies; we depend on things being constant or the same. Whereas, if your closet is still the same size as it was the last time you saw it, and if jumbo jets are generally still the same size, then your probability of it being to big to fit will still be valid, which means your thinking is based on those constants.  It is this type of tabulations and calculations which permit us to refer to ourselves as being stable.  Can you imagine what we'd be like if our environment changed without us being aware.  We'd be stone crazy.

When belief is taken to another level wherein the element of reliance and confidence is brought into play, then we generally refer to that level of belief as faith. Does faith have a definition or is it just synonymous with belief?

When we talk about faith, we are dealing with a level of trust, confidence, reliance or dependence. Do we believe the earth is going to turn into the light of the sun tomorrow? I could have said: will the sun rise tomorrow, which isn't true, because the sun doesn't move; so will the earth turn into the light of the sun tomorrow? Most would say yes, which is not as important as why we believe that. Do we rely on that? Do we trust that this phenomena of the "sun rising" will take place? Do we have confidence that that's going to take place? Do we depend upon it being so? This is part of us understanding what faith is.

If I were to stick my hand in fire, would it burn? Suppose I told you that only happened in 1995 and as of 1996, hands don't burn in fire anymore? I probably could show you an example of a man walking across burning coals or a fire breather blowing fire out of his mouth in an effort to unravel your confidence that fire will burn hands, etc....

What if I had paralysis, or deadness in my whole arm and put it into fire, would I get burned? YES, because regardless if whether or not I can feel it, the process of burning is still taking place. Why? Because as fire is still rapid oxidation and the hand or arm is still flesh, the reaction will still be materially the same, which we call burning! What am I getting at? You can rely or rest assured that as fire is still composed or made up of that which God created it to be, and when something comes in contact with it, the reaction will be the same. Why do we rely on the consistency of the process? Are we sure, and if so, on what basis does that surety rests? Being a believer is one thing, but being one of the faithful is a bit different. There is more of a trust, confidence and dependence factor involved. Please stick with me.

What makes us trust that the earth will turn into the light of the sun, or what makes us have confidence, or what makes us rely on that is its history of having done that for so long! Think about it. We have been experiencing this history at least since we have been on the planet-right! In fact, we take it for granted, so much so, that many of us have all but threw away any notion of wondering or thinking about it anymore.

Do we not take for granted that when we bite down in an orange that the vitamin C we have come to expect to be there will in fact be there? Not only do we take for granted that the vitamin C will be in the orange, but we take it another level in assuming that the vitamin C will nourish our bodies! Although we don't necessarily see it happening; we don't smell it happening; we don't taste it happening; nor do we feel it happening! If our liver decided that it wanted to protest and go on strike, you and I would be in serious trouble, but there is a supreme reliance on the Creator, Who created us as creatures, that if we put vegetation, fruits and grains in our bodies, these elements (foods) will nourish our organs and perpetuate our lives! This is faith based on verifiable history.

When we say we trust that our respective location will turn into the light of the sun tomorrow, that's faith; when we say that we trust that the air we breath through our mouths or nostril will furnish oxygen for our lungs, that's faith; when we assume that vitamin C is in an orange and it will nourish my organs, that's faith; and it is defined as history.  Thus faith is reliance based on verifiable history.  It happens over and over and over.

Many of us who draw our information from this world's schools, colleges and universities have been taught and have come to merely believe that history is those occurrences which have happened in the past.  This is not entirely true.  Sociology deals with following, analyzing and predicting patterns within a society.  Now, when an overall platform is consistent, or a societal circumstance is predictable, modifications and manipulation can be injected to control results.  These are the type of experiments that social scientists occupy themselves with.

## Is Elijah Muhammad the Offspring of Garvey & Drew Ali?

An example of how this plays out is when the people are metered by their socio-economic-status.  Where the family lives, what type of money the father makes and the type of schooling and training he has, are the determining factors, which western social scientists use to project what his children will do and be able to do for years to come; in fact, have done an interestingly thorough job.  They have actually been able to set up a system based on economics, status and education, which are consistent markers to determine if one can "make it" in this society, for to be unqualified or lacking in any one of them, automatically means your offspring is doomed.  You may have noticed that as far back as the early 1980's, students applying for college entrance and financial aid were asked questions like, "Are you the first one in your family to attend college?" This was for the real purpose of adjusting their system, although we were made to believe otherwise.  What are we getting at?

If the social scientist of today can study the people, under a consistent system, and project what the people's offspring are going to be doing decades from now, what can men supremely qualified in the science of the universal laws of creation do?  Is not the laws of creation more consistent that the so-called principles which Western World societies have been and are still based on?  As we have been basing our lifestyles and confidence on their system, we may have forgotten about the universal system above, around and within us, a natural system which we have been taking for granted!

Is not the Holy Qur'an and Bible composed of projections which we call prophecies.  Do not these books contain occurrences which are said to have happened and are predicted to happen?  Did these books fall out of the sky or have there been human beings who have made these strikingly accurate projections?

Is it coincidental that all of the symbolism of both books is enveloped and clothed in natural elements or elements of nature ranging from the celestial bodies to the very insects under our feet and over our heads. The sun, moon, stars, goats, sheep, lion, bees, ants, trees, snakes, etc.... As this is so, we cannot separate these books and their content from the same creator and His laws and principles on which we have relied all of our lives, and that's regardless of who we are or where we live. All to say that for you to utter that you don't believe in the truths of either of these books would be to deny the very elements you have been relying on your whole existence and are still relying on for your existence. Some may be attempting to wiggle and squirm while you are wrestling with my premise, but as you breathe the breath to do so, you are still bearing witness despite yourself.

In one of 40 questions and answers which Master Fard Muhammad gave to Elijah Muhammad in a "second term examination," it reads, "Who wrote the Holy Qur'an or Bible? Will you tell us why does Islam renew her history every twenty-five thousand years?

Answer: The Holy Qur'an or Bible is made by the Original people, Who is Allah, the Supreme Being or Black Man of Asia. The

Qur'an will expire in the year twenty-five thousand, nine thousand and eighty years from the date of this writing (from approximately 1934). The Nation of Islam is all wise and does everything right and exact. The Planet Earth, which is the home of Islam, is approximately twenty-five thousand miles in circumference, so the wise man of the East (Black Man) makes history or Qur'an to equal his home circumference: a year to every mile and thus, every time his history last twenty-five thousand years, he renews it for another twenty-five thousand years. What does this question and answer mean?

To begin with, the question tells us that someone physical wrote both books and that Islam has something to do with this. What is Islam? Islam is the total submission to the Will of the Creator. Why didn't I say Allah? When we understand comparative religions, we come to understand that within each, the "God" of the respective religion raised up or sent His representative for the respective work among that given people; whereas, that prophet or messenger had to relate God's message in the language of the people to whom he was sent; therefore, he would call God's name according to what the people's language was; thus, the different names of God: Elohim, Yahweh, Jehovah, etc.... Yet, as both books prophesy, in the "last days," we would see God as He really is. Why? Because before Elijah Muhammad, none of the messengers had seen God, which is why the peoples of the earth thought God was a spirit.

According to the afore-said prophesy, when God manifested Himself in the "last days," He came in a form in order for the people to see Him as He is." But, what I am driving at is that in the last days, God would have a name that would include all the names by which He has been represented and that name is Allah, which simply means the All In All. So when one says the name Allah, they are simply saying all the names of God at once. Why is this so important? When the term Islam is used, we are simply talking about a state of being. Islam means peace and its significance means the making of peace; therefore, when the planets rotate in harmony, they derive a state of peace. When the elements in nature act in accord with each other, it produces a state of peace, because all elements are turning one way which is where the term universe comes from. Uni comes from Latin, which means one  and verse comes from Latin as well, which means vertere: to turn.   When put together, they mean to turn one direction or with oneness.  The state produced as a result of turning in oneness is called peace in the English language and Islam in the Arabic language.  So, when one compliments the consistencies of nature or the natural laws of the universe, one is actually bearing witness to the state produced, which is peace or Islam.

This state is renewed every twenty-five thousand years.  As the answer goes on, it states that the two books, Qur'an or Bible is made by the original people, how?  Similar to the way that the present day social scientists renew their programs to rule you and me.  Their knowledge is limited, which is why their societies are corrupt and flawed, but the original Black people base their society and the ruling of their societies on the natural laws and principles governing our planet, which is why they can project according to the turning and circumference (the distance going around in a complete circle) of our planet. It is the consistency and reliance based on the planet never changing or deviating, which gives us confidence in making accurate calculations as to what can happen and what can't. If there is something we don't want to happen, we have wise scientists who can manipulate various elements in our universe to alter events for our best interest. This is why the prophesies in the books will take place, because the basis on which they rest is on the same system that you and I take for granted, but never has failed us yet. The natural laws of the universe are the foundation for the books, and the fathers of the Original Black people are the ones who wrote them - our Fathers. The circumference of our planet is 24, 896 miles. Approximately 25,000 miles. 24 scientist write our history. 23 do the writing and it is then brought to the 24th and He acts as

Judge to determine what will come to pass and what won't. This 24th one is called Allah, the Supreme Being. Notice He is called the Supreme "Being," this is because He is human like you and I. The difference is that He is The Wisest Human. All of us have some wisdom and since we as black people are direct descendants or offspring of God, we are all Allah, it's just that there is One wiser than us all and this is what makes Him Supreme. How this will factor into Master Fard Muhammad's coming will be discussed in forthcoming chapters; however, my intent here is to show that the very books which the "critics" don't use in the "explaining" of Master Fard Muhammad, is the primary tool necessary for explaining!

This perspective is thus submitted in order to make this ultimate point. As we have demonstrated that the writers who sought to "explain" Master Fard Muhammad, Elijah Muhammad and The Nation of Islam are in fact unqualified to explain, because: 1) They manifested their own ignorance when it came to the origin of Master Fard Muhammad; therefore, any one coming in

His name or using Him as the standard of measurement for their action, is beyond the comprehension of many previous writers; 2) The Messenger of Allah, Elijah Muhammad, said throughout his mission, which came strictly from Master Fard Muhammad, Who Elijah Muhammad said is God in Person and that the origin, aims and purpose of Allah (God), Master Fard Muhammad, is clearly in the scriptures, both Holy Qur'an and Bible; then if previous writers don't use the scriptures as their basis for explaining, defining or analyzing Master Fard Muhammad, then quite frankly, it's like using a chocolate cake recipe as a standard of measurement for a plumber; and 3) If they don't use the scriptures as the basis for determining if He is Who He says He is, or Who Elijah Muhammad says that Master Fard Muhammad or he himself is, then all their writings have been a supreme exercise in futility all the time!

As many have borne witness to the profound changes that have occurred as a direct result of Messenger Elijah Muhammad's works, the profound changes experienced by black people in America, and the unmatched affect he has demonstrated on the world, then one must bear witness to the fact that regardless of what others may have said about who Master Fard Muhammad is or isn't, no doubt that as Elijah has always said that his instruction came from Master Fard Muhammad, indeed Elijah Muhammad and his followers have most surely gotten the most benefit from his coming and presence, which stands to reason that Elijah Muhammad is the most qualified to explain who He Is!

"If I do not the works of my Father, believe me not.  But if I do, though ye believe not me, believe the works: that ye may know, and believe, that the Father [is] in me, and I in him." (John 10:38)

My advice to the hasty, ill-informed writers, critics and hypocrites is to calculate on Elijah Muhammad's works when attempting to ascertain who it is that he represents.  For you need to KNOW the Father of his work in order to KNOW if he did the work; for most surely if Noble Drew Ali or Marcus

Garvey were his fathers, then surely, according to the words of Jesus, Elijah Muhammad would have done the same thing they did, and what Drew and Garvey had in common is that neither lasted too long; therefore, had he used what they used, he wouldn't have lasted as long as forty (40) years; likewise, even if you still don't want to accept what Elijah Muhammad said over forty (40) years, regarding the origin of Master Fard Muhammad, then there stands his irrefutable works still looking us in the face at this late date.

Perhaps if they would analyze it closer, without bias, they may come to believe the works which may help them come to KNOW and believe that which they have been puzzled about, unable to explain, incapable of properly interpreting and seeing darkly, and that is the Father of what Elijah Muhammad and the Nation is all about: Allah (God), Who Came in the person of Master Fard Muhammad.

I can not deny that the Honorable Elijah Muhammad admired both Noble

Drew Ali and Marcus Garvey.  Ali was the first Black man to make an attempt at bringing Islam to the Black man and woman in America and a great teacher was he.  No one can deny the grand and noble work of Marcus Garvey; yet, the truth is, if you study the actual facts taught by the Honorable Elijah Muhammad, you don't see that in the writings of Marcus Garvey or in the writings of Nobel Drew Ali.  Teachings like: What is the square miles of the Planet Earth?  How much is the land?  How much is the water?  What are the exact square miles of the useful land that is used every day by the total population of the Planet Earth?  What is the distance of the Sun to the Earth?  What is the distance of Mercury to the Sun?  What is the circumference of the Universe?  What is the diameter of the Sun?  What is the temperature of the Sun?  Marcus Garvey and Nobel Ali didn't teach this!

The Bible said that when God came, He would measure the Earth and the water and He would tell us what the earth weighed and what the measurement of the Earth is.  Garvey and Ali didn't teach this; in fact,

## Is Elijah Muhammad the Offspring of Garvey & Drew Ali?

Sigmund Freud didn't teach this; Plato didn't teach it, prophet Muhammad of Arabia didn't teach it; the Holy Qur'an did not mention it and the Bible did not teach it. The Bible only said that when God came, He would give us the measurements of the Earth and the universe. Why? Because God knows the square miles, the inches. He knows how much water is in the oceans, plants, animals and atmosphere. So through Elijah Muhammad, He taught us the square mileage of the Earth: How much is land and how much is water. He taught us the square miles of the islands, planet and our universe.

It is not strange to scholars of Elijah Muhammad that white scholars had begun to approximate their figure in their encyclopedias and books of science to those figures taught by Elijah Muhammad, Messenger of Allah.

The question must be asked, how long has the white man been making progress? Look at his information explosion on his (information highway). Since When did white people learn how to crack and split atoms?  Who taught it?  Where did they get it?  When did white people learn how to go into the genetic make-up of a thing, to correct things that needed correction?  Elijah Muhammad was teaching this before they even found the magic bullet to challenge polio!

You see, we who are authentic, sincerely followers of Elijah Muhammad are not fools.  Wisdom is known of it children.  If we are wise, it is because of Elijah Muhammad only.  We were not produced by Yale, USC, Princeton, Harvard or Howard!

It was from Elijah Muhammad, Messenger of Allah, who taught us how to use language and was actually given and English Lesson.  This knowledge enables us to not only excite the imagination and stirs the consciousness of our people, but he taught us how to seed and feed the unconscious mind.

When Elijah Muhammad, Messenger of Allah, taught us of the weight of an atom and the fact that of how God created

Himself, where in the writings of Garvey and Ali could that be found?  When Elijah Muhammad, Messenger of Allah, taught us of the speed and the power of thought, where in the writings of Garvey or Ali did these men teach this?  When Elijah Muhammad, Messenger of Allah, taught us of tuning in on another persons thinking, where in the writings of Garvey and Ali was this supreme science taught?

When Elijah Muhammad, Messenger of Allah taught us about the Earth and the moon, that the white man had to go to the moon to find out if it was true.  But who sent him there?  What gave him the thought that he could even go there?

When this white man was inspired to go into his laboratories to study the life germ under the telescope and advance to the stage of cutting out this or that from the chromosome that he didn't like, where did he get this knowledge from?  He didn't get it out the Bible, nor did he read it from the Holy Qur'an.  He got if from the teachings of Elijah Muhammad when he taught about their (white people's) origin.  When Elijah Muhammad taught about their father, Yakub, they began to study it.  Although they made the common man, as well as the ignorant Muslim, believe that it was a made-up fairy tale, they are now eliminating diseases in people before they are even born.  All from the teachings of Elijah Muhammad.  Now I ask once again, DID GARVEY OR ALI TEACH THIS?

Many called Elijah Muhammad's teaching fantastic, and far-fetched when he taught of the white race's father, Yakub.  They called it foolishness when he taught of the white race's origin.  Marcus Garvey and Noble Drew Ali didn't teach that; in fact, Moses didn't teach it, Jesus didn't teach it, prophet Muhammad didn't teach it, and there is not a scholar on the planet, black or white, who has come forward to make Elijah Muhammad, Messenger of Allah out of a liar!

When Elijah Muhammad asked the world: "WHO IS THE ORIGINAL MAN?" Marcus Garvey didn't asked that question!

## Is Elijah Muhammad the Offspring of Garvey & Drew Ali?

Nobel Drew Ali didn't ask that question! Jesus didn't ask that question! Moses didn't ask that question!

Where in the writings of Garvey and Ali can you find how the other planets were made? Where in the writings of Garvey and Ali can you find the science of microbes? Where in the writings of Garvey and Ali can you find the weight of the Earth? Where in their writings can you find why the moon is of the same materials of the Earth and the moon's affect on the life-blood of our nation? Where in their writings can you find the term Asiatic?

For those of afro-centric and nationalistic thought, you never heard of this term until Elijah Muhammad taught that the whole planet was called Asia and we were Asiatic Black people. You thought is was talking about another land mass where yellow and brown people lived. Surely if Garvey knew he was an original Asiatic Blackman, he would not have referred to himself and his organization as Negroes.

I could go on endlessly pointing out the shear fact that as great and noble both, Noble Drew Ali and Marcus Garvey are, it is easier putting a camel through the eye of a needle than to prove that Elijah Muhammad was a continuation of either of these men.

It is becoming very fashionable to promote that Elijah Muhammad had a legacy or knowledge passed down to him by Garvey and/or Ali, especially when attempting to give some kind of intellectual continuity to the Black Experience here in America. In a vain effort to shore up decade old theories and guesses about our identity and origin, many afro-centric and nationalistic theorists have found it very convenient; yet factually deficient, to link Elijah Muhammad with Garvey and Ali. They believe that by perpetuating that Elijah Muhammad merely had handed down teachings, it would in affect give legitimacy to their dead-in-the-water dinosaur schools of thought, take credit for the greatest work to have ever been witnessed on our planet and refute Elijah Muhammad's claim of being a Messenger of God simultaneously.

No one is attempting to take credit from Garvey and Ali.  My attempt is to help set the record straight with facts.  How the true followers of Elijah Muhammad feel about these untruths doesn't seem to bother the advocates; therefore, very little, if any, is reciprocated.  There is no such thing of a legacy of Elijah Muhammad from Garvey or Ali.  We must force those who advocate that Elijah Muhammad got his teachings passed down to him from Marcus Garvey and Noble Drew Ali to either prove it or be condemned as liars and enemies of God, His Messenger and the Believers!

Minister Nasir Makr Hakim, Founder
Messenger Elijah Muhammad
Propagation Society

# Is Elijah Muhammad the Offspring of Garvey & Drew Ali?

Made in the USA
Monee, IL
07 July 2026